ACCA

Financial Reporting (FR)

Pocket Notes

British library cataloguing-in-publication data

A catalogue record for this book is available from the British Library.

Published by:
Kaplan Publishing UK
Unit 2 The Business Centre
Molly Millars Lane
Wokingham
Berkshire
RG41 2QZ

ISBN 978-1-83996-415-2

© Kaplan Financial Limited, 2023

Printed and bound in Great Britain.

Acknowledgements

This product contains copyright material and trademarks of the IFRS Foundation®. All rights reserved. Used under licence from the IFRS Foundation®. Reproduction and use rights are strictly limited. For more information about the IFRS Foundation and rights to use its material please visit www.ifrs.org.

IFRS

Trade Marks

Contents

Chapter 1: Published accounts 1

Chapter 2: Tangible non-current assets 9

Chapter 3: Intangible assets 19

Chapter 4: Impairment of assets 25

Chapter 5: Non-current assets held for sale and discontinued operations 29

Chapter 6: The regulatory and conceptual framework 33

Chapter 7: Conceptual framework – measurement 45

Chapter 8: Other Standards 49

Chapter 9: Financial assets and financial liabilities 55

Chapter 10: Foreign currency transactions 61

Chapter 11: Revenue 65

Chapter 12: Leases 69

Chapter 13: Taxation 75

Chapter 14: Earnings per share 79

Chapter 15: Provisions, contingent liabilities and contingent assets.................................. 83

Chapter 16: Statement of cash flows 89

Chapter 17: Principles of consolidated financial statements.. 97

Chapter 18: Consolidated statement of financial position 101

Chapter 19: Consolidated statement of profit or loss 113

Chapter 20: Associates.. 121

Chapter 21: Disposals 127

Chapter 22: Interpretation of financial statements 131

References: R.1

Index: I.1

This document references IFRS® Standards and IAS® Standards, which are authored by the International Accounting Standards Board (the Board), and published in the 2022 IFRS Standards Red Book.

KAPLAN PUBLISHIN

The exam

The exam is structured as follows:

		Number of marks
Section A	15 objective test questions, being a mix of calculations and explanations	30
Section B	3 objective case questions, each consisting of 5 objective test questions	30
Section C	2 questions examining the interpretation and preparation of financial statement for a single entity or a group	40 (2x20)

The computer-based exam (CBE) is three hours long.

All questions are **compulsory**.

The objective test questions will test all areas of the syllabus. The mix of explanations and calculations may mean that the calculations can be quite technical, despite being relatively small.

Revision

- Practise consolidations and accounts preparation until you can do them quickly and accurately to time without fail.

- Use these Pocket Notes to give yourself a broad and thorough knowledge and understanding of the whole syllabus. This will ensure that you have the ability to score well on the other questions.

- In the exam, make sure you attempt all the questions. This is a very time pressured exam and you may need to leave a question unfinished and move on in order to do this. Many students fail each year because they only complete some questions and it wasn't enough to gain a pass.

Quality and accuracy are of the utmost importance to us so if you spot an error in any of our products, please send an email to mykaplanreporting@kaplan.com with full details, or follow the link to the feedback form in MyKaplan.

Our Quality Co-ordinator will work with our technical team to verify the error and take action to ensure it is corrected in future editions.

1

Published accounts

In this chapter

- IAS 1 Presentation of financial statements.

IAS 1 Presentation of financial statements

One of the 20 mark questions in section C

Statement of profit or loss and other comprehensive income

The following format is an extract from the appendix to IAS 1. It shows a model statement of profit or loss and other comprehensive income for a single entity.

Statement of profit or loss and other comprehensive income

	$
Revenue	X
Cost of sales	(X)
Gross profit	X
Distribution costs	(X)
Administrative expenses	(X)
Profit from operations	(X)
Finance costs	(X)
Investment income	X
Profit before tax	X
Tax expense	(X)
Profit for the period	X
Other comprehensive income	
Gains/losses on property revaluation	X
Total comprehensive income for the year	X

Statement of financial position

As before, this format is for a single entity.

ASSETS	$
Non-Current Assets	
Property, plant and equipment	X
Intangible assets	X
Investments	X
	X
Current Assets	
Inventories	X
Trade receivables	X
Cash and cash equivalents	X
	X
Total assets	X

EQUITY AND LIABILITIES	
Equity	
Share capital	X
Other components of equity	X
Retained earnings	X
Total equity	X
Non-current liabilities	
Long-term borrowings	X
Deferred tax	X
Long-term provisions	X
	X
Current liabilities	
Trade and other payables	X
Overdraft	X
Current tax payable	X
Short-term provisions	X
	X
Total liabilities	X
Total equity and liabilities	X

The secret to questions involving the preparation of financial statements is practice, followed by more practice.

Key Point

If you attempt as many of these questions as you possibly can while studying and revising for the exam then you will find that the preparation becomes second nature.

Don't worry if you make the odd slip of presentation or layout.

Exam focus

The main reason for knowing the IAS 1 formats well is that they will enable you to attempt questions quickly and efficiently.

Statement of changes in equity

This shows the movements on reserves for the period under consideration.

Again, practice makes perfect.

Statement of changes in equity (SOCIE)

	Share capital	Share premium	Revaluation surplus	Retained earnings	Equity option	Total
Opening balance	X	X	X	X		X
Change in accounting policy/ errors (IAS 8)				(X)		(X)
Share issue	X	X				X
Revaluation surplus/deficit			X/(X)			X/(X)
Equity option					X	X
Profit from SPL				X		X
Dividends				(X)		(X)
Transfer to retained earnings			(X)	X		
Closing balance	X	X	X	X	X	X

Question approach

1 Read requirement, set up answer and workings

- Cost of sales
- Property, plant and equipment
- Deferred tax

2 Line by line down TB/draft FSs
  – every number goes somewhere!

3 Adjustments – 2 effects, debit and credit

4 Complete workings

Exam focus

Exam standard questions on this area can be found in the exam kit as follows:

Constructed response questions:

- June 2009 – Pricewell
- June 2012 – Fresco
- December 2012 – Quincy
- December 2013 – Moby
- December 2014 – Kandy
- Sep/Dec 2015 – Moston

Underpinning question practice

To practise the basics use the following test your understandings:

- Study Text
  Chapter 1
  Test your understanding 1 and 2
- Chapter 24
  Test your understanding 1 to 5

2

Tangible non-current assets

In this chapter

- IAS 16.
- IAS 23.
- IAS 20.
- IAS 40.

IAS 16

Exam focus

Questions at this level are as likely to ask you to explain and justify the rules in the relevant IAS as to ask you to apply those rules.

IAS 16 Property, plant and equipment deals with most of the issues associated with non-current assets.

Is it an asset?

One of the biggest problems that arises in the real world is the decision as to whether an item of expenditure was to acquire a non-current asset or whether it should be treated as an expense.

Exam focus

Questions might test your ability to distinguish between asset and expense items.

IAS 16 provides some pointers, although these often don't give a clear and definitive treatment.

> **Initial measurement**

Include:
Directly attributable costs in getting asset into working condition for its intended use, e.g.
- Purchase price
- Improvement costs
- Commissioning and testing

Assets under construction
- Labour costs
- Site clearance
- Installation costs
- Professional fees

Exclude:
- Costs incurred after asset is ready for use but not yet being used.
- Repair/ maintenance costs
- Early settlement discounts

Subsequent expenditure

Any subsequent expenditure on existing property, plant and equipment should only be capitalised if it improves an asset's revenue earning capacity, e.g. capitalise an extension to a building but not decoration costs.

Depreciation

Definition

Depreciation is the systematic allocation of the depreciable amount of an asset over its useful life.

Exam focus

Read the question carefully, the examiner will tell you how depreciation is to be calculated.

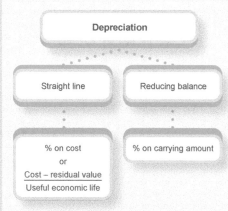

All non-current assets with finite useful lives must be depreciated.

Assets should be depreciated over their remaining lives, whether they are shown at cost less depreciation to date or at a valuation.

- Check useful life (UL) , residual value (RV) and method annually and revise if necessary

- Changes to UL :

New dep$_n$ charge $= \dfrac{\text{CA @ date of change} - \text{RV}}{\text{revised 'remaining' UL}}$

Disposals _____

When asset disposed of must calculate the accounting profit or loss on disposal and remove the asset cost and accumulated depreciation from the statement of financial position.

To find profit or loss on disposal in the exam compare:

Disposal proceeds	X
Carrying amount (CA)	(X)
Profit/loss on disposal	X

If proceeds > CA = profit.
If proceeds < CA = loss

Revaluations

The mechanics of revaluation are very straightforward.

- Restate the cost/valuation to the revalued amount.
- Restate the accumulated depreciation on the asset to zero.
- The net increase/decrease is the gain/ loss on revaluation.

A **gain on revaluation** is credited to the revaluation surplus (via the statement of changes in equity and disclosed as other comprehensive income).

A **loss on revaluation** is usually[1] charged to the statement of profit or loss as an expense.

Depreciation is subsequently based on the revalued amount.

If a company decides to show one asset at valuation then it is required to revalue all of the assets in that category (e.g. all land and

buildings). This is to prevent companies from 'cherry-picking' assets that have increased in value to be shown at valuation while leaving those that would have decreased at their cost less depreciation.

Once a category of assets has been revalued then the valuations have to be kept reasonably up to date.

Exam focus

In the exam pay attention to the revaluation date. The answer will vary depending on whether revaluation takes place at the beginning or end of the year.

---

[1] If the asset had previously been revalued at a gain then part of any subsequent loss on revaluation can be deducted from the revaluation surplus, up to the amount that had previously been credited in respect of the asset.

IAS 23

IAS 23 Borrowing costs deals with the question of whether finance costs incurred in the construction of a building can be capitalised.

Borrowing costs must be capitalised as part of the cost of the asset, if that asset is one which '**necessarily takes a substantial period of time to get ready for its intended use or sale**' (IAS 23, para 5) i.e. it is a qualifying asset.

Commence capitalisation of borrowing costs when:

- Expenditure being incurred
- Borrowing being incurred
- Work commenced.

Capitalisation should be stopped when asset is ready for use or if construction is suspended.

IAS 20

IAS 20 Accounting for government grants and disclosure of government assistance deals with grants, which are provided by government in respect of capital or revenue expenditure.

Revenue grants

(e.g. a government contribution towards the cost of wages) can **either**:

- be presented as a credit in the statement of profit or loss **or**
- be deducted from the related expense.

Capital grants

(e.g. a government contribution towards the cost of a new piece of machinery)

Capital grants presentation choice:

- Net grant off cost of asset
- Depreciate reduced amount

- Capitalise/depreciate asset as normal.
- Treat grant as deferred income.
- Release grant income to the statement of profit or loss over the asset's useful life.
- Applies the matching concept to the grant

You are free to choose whichever treatment you deem more appropriate (or simpler), unless the examiner specifies a particular treatment for a grant.

IAS 40

IAS 40 Investment properties excludes certain properties from the requirement that all non-current assets with finite lives be depreciated.

Investment property is land or a building '**held to earn rentals, or for capital appreciation or both**' (IAS 40, para 5), rather than for use in the enterprise or for sale in the ordinary course of business.

Owner-occupied property is excluded from the definition of investment property.

Investment properties should initially be measured at cost.

IAS 40 then gives a choice between following:

Accounting choice

Cost model:
- Capitalise at cost
- Depreciate as normal

Fair value model:
- Capitalise at cost
- Each year revalue to fair value
- Gain/loss via statement of profit or loss - not revaluation surplus
- No depreciation

Exam standard questions on this area can
be found in the exam kit as follows:

Objective case questions:

- Q226 – 235
- Q246 – 265

Underpinning question practice

To practise the basics use the following test
your understandings:

- Study Text – Chapter 2
- Test your understanding 1 – 11

**Review of useful lives, residual values
and method**

3

Intangible assets

In this chapter

- IAS 38.

IAS 38

IAS 38 Intangible assets deals with similar issues to those raised by IAS 16.

Key Point

The main difference between tangible and intangible assets from an accounting point of view is that the recognition criteria for intangibles are more complex and the determination of useful lives can be equally problematic.

Definition

'**An intangible asset is an identifiable non-monetary asset without physical substance**' (IAS 38, para 8).

In order to capitalise an intangible asset it must satisfy the following criteria:

- identifiable
- controlled by the entity
- future economic benefits are probable
- capable of reliable measurement.

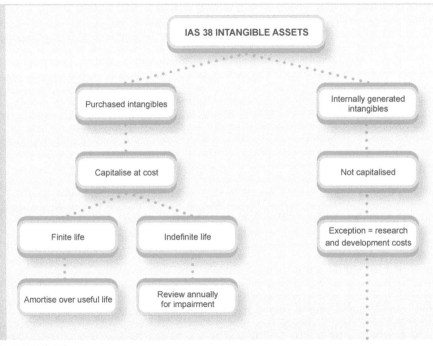

Research

Development

Expense immediately

*P*robable flow of benefit
*I*ntention to complete
*R*eliable measure
*A*dequate resources
*T*echnically feasible
*E*xpected to be profitable

Amortise when commercial production begins

Review annually to ensure criteria still met. If not – expense immediately

KAPLAN PUBLISHING

Exam standard questions on this area can be found in the exam kit as follows:

Objective case questions:

- Q271 – 275

Underpinning question practice

To practise the basics use the following test your understandings:

- Study Text – Chapter 3

  Test your understanding 1

  Test your understanding 2

  Test your understanding 3

4

Impairment of assets

In this chapter

- IAS 36.

IAS 36

IAS 36 Impairment of assets is intended to avoid the possibility that non-current assets (whether tangible or intangible) are carried at excessive amounts in the statement of financial position.

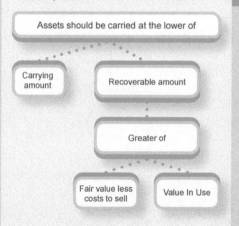

Assets should be carried at the lower of

Carrying amount

Recoverable amount

Greater of

Fair value less costs to sell

Value In Use

Indications of impairment

- Operating losses
- Technological advancements
- Obsolescence/physical damage.

Key Point

Impairment losses are charged to the statement of profit or loss, except to the extent that they reverse a previously-recognised gain on revaluation, in which case that part will go to the revaluation surplus.

Summary of accounting

Dr Impairment expense
Cr Non-current asset

Unless previously revalued

Dr Revaluation surplus
Dr Impairment expense
Cr Non-current asset

Cash generating units

- A cash generating unit (CGU) is the smallest group of identifiable assets that generate independent cash flows.
- An impairment loss on a CGU occurs when a revenue stream is damaged.
- Allocate impairment loss with the following write down rules:

    1. Goodwill allocated to CGU

    2. Remaining assets (pro-rata over carrying amount)

	Carrying amount	Impairment	Recoverable amount
Goodwill	X	(X)	X
Other assets	X	(X)	X
	—	—	—
	X	(X)	X
	—	—	—

Exam standard questions on this area can be found in the exam kit as follows:

Objective case questions:

- Q276 – 280

Underpinning question practice

To practise the basics use the following test your understandings:

- Study Text – Chapter 4

    Test your understanding 1

    Test your understanding 2

    Test your understanding 3

    Test your understanding 4

    Test your understanding 5

5

Non-current assets held for sale and discontinued operations

In this chapter

- IFRS 5 – Non-current assets held for sale.
- Discontinued operations.

IFRS 5 Non-current assets held for sale

A non-current asset should be classified as 'held for sale' '**if its carrying amount will be recovered principally through a sale transaction rather than through continuing use**' (IFRS 5, para 6).

Reclassify a non-current asset to a current asset 'held for sale' when the following criteria are met:

- asset must be available for immediate sale in its present condition
- the sale must be highly probable, meaning that:
  - management are committed to a plan to sell the asset
  - there is an active programme to locate a buyer, and
  - the asset is being actively marketed

- the sale is expected to be completed within 12 months of its classification as held for sale
- it is unlikely that the plan will be significantly changed or withdrawn.

Once an asset is classified as 'held for sale' it is no longer depreciated.

Non-current assets that qualify as held for sale should be measured:

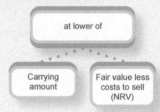

Impact – losses recognised on reclassification but gains are not (i.e. impairment recorded in the statement of profit or loss – gains not taken to a revaluation surplus).

Chapter 5

Discontinued operations

'A discontinued operation is a component of an entity that either has been disposed of, or is classified as held for sale, and:

- **represents a separate major line of business or geographical area of operations**
- **is part of a single co-ordinated plan to dispose of a separate major line of business or geographical area of operations, or**
- **is a subsidiary acquired exclusively with a view to resale**' (IFRS 5, para 32).

Discontinued operations are required to be shown separately in the statement of profit or loss in order to help users to predict future performance, i.e. based upon continuing operations.

Exam focus

Exam standard questions on this area can be found in the exam kit as follows:

Objective case questions:

- Q281 – 283

Underpinning question practice

To practise the basics use the following test your understandings:

- Study Text – Chapter 5

  Test your understanding 1

  Test your understanding 2

  Test your understanding 3

  Test your understanding 4

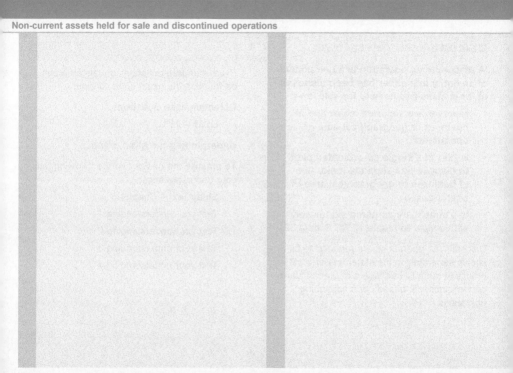

6

The regulatory and conceptual framework

In this chapter

- The standard setting system.
- The regulatory framework.
- Principles-based v rules based accounting.
- Not-for-profit and public sector entities.
- What is a conceptual framework.
- Contents of the framework.

The standard setting system

Accounting standards are necessary in order to enable companies to produce financial statements that are relatively consistent. This makes it easier for readers to understand and interpret financial statements.

Accounting standards are set by the accountancy profession. The most important aspect of the standard setting process occurs at the international level.

The most important body for our purposes is the International Accounting Standards Board (the Board).

The IFRS Foundation
Responsible for governance of the standard setting process.

The Board
Responsible for setting IFRS ® Standards.

ISSB
Aims to deliver comprehensive sustainability-related disclosure.

IFRIC
Issues rapid guidance on accounting matters where divergent interpretations of IFRS Standards have arisen.

IFRS AC
Forum for experts from different countries and different business sectors to offer advice to the Board.

Accounting standards

The Board sets standards in the form of International Financial Reporting Standards.

The IFRS Interpretations Committee (IFRIC) deals with loopholes that arise in existing standards.

Many IFRS Standards are examinable in this paper.

The IFRIC interpretations are not examinable.

The Standards generally do not have any direct legal status. In most countries it is a legal requirement that financial statements 'present fairly' or give a 'true and fair view'.

In practice, IFRS standards and IFRIC Interpretations provide a basis for external auditors and other regulators to assess the extent to which the standards comply with these criteria.

Setting standards

Standards are set by a process of consultation.

The Board identifies a subject and establishes an advisory committee to recommend an appropriate treatment.

Each standard is preceded by an exposure draft, which gives the public the opportunity to comment.

At any stage the Board might issue a discussion paper.

Key Point

National standard setting bodies

The Board works in partnership with the major national standard setting bodies.

All the major national standard setters are represented on the Board and their views are taken into account so that a consensus can be reached.

The regulatory framework

Users of financial statements must be able to rely on them for decision making purposes. There is a wide range of users who rely heavily on financial statements.

The preparation of accounts for publication is affected by a range of rules and regulations in addition to IFRS Standards. These include:

- national company law

- EU directives (which provide a framework for company law within the EU)
- stock exchange rules.

Principles-based v rules-based accounting

There is a major debate in the US about the role of rules v principles in accounting regulation.

Principles-based accounting involves preparing financial statements so that they meet a set of principle-based criteria. For example, UK financial statements must give a 'true and fair view'.

Rules-based accounting puts the requirement to comply with each individual accounting standard first. This has been the case, for example, in the US. This approach has been blamed for the problems that arose in the case of Enron, where the auditors knew that the financial statements were potentially misleading, but could do nothing about it because they complied with all the rules.

The main difference between principles-based and rules-based accounting is that the former has a "true and fair override", which means that it is not only possible, but mandatory to ignore the rules if doing so is required in order to avoid producing misleading financial statements.

Not-for-profit and public sector entities

The corporate objectives of businesses are very different from those of not-for-profit and public sector entities.

Companies exist largely to make profits. They have a range of stakeholders, the most important of whom is generally the body of shareholders. Financial statements are intended to communicate the profitability and viability of the business.

Not-for-profit and public sector entities do not exist to make profits, but they do have a diverse range of stakeholders, many of whom have a legitimate interest in the body's financial stewardship.

In practice, the accounting policies adopted by not-for-profit and public sector entities are increasingly similar. For example, government bodies generally have to produce the equivalent of an income statement and statement of financial position and these are prepared in much the same way as they would be for a business.

What is a conceptual framework?

A conceptual framework is:

- a coherent system of interrelated objectives and fundamental principles
- a framework which prescribes the nature, function and limits of financial accounting and financial statements.

Without a conceptual framework (CF) standard setters will find it difficult to produce accounting standards that are consistent with one another.

Key Point

It is difficult to decide on the most appropriate treatment of a problem issue 'from first principles' without first establishing what those principles are.

The Board has a conceptual framework document.

This document is on the list of Board publications that is examinable.

The Framework should be the starting point for any Board working party that has been asked to comment on or make suggestions for any problem that has arisen with existing standards. Amongst other things, it sets out the user groups and their information requirements and proposes in outline how best to satisfy those needs.

Contents of the framework

Exam focus

You should have a broad understanding of the contents of the Framework. You might have to explain the logic behind an accounting standard and the Framework will provide you with a sound basis for doing so.

The Framework contains the following chapters:

- the objective of financial reporting

- qualitative characteristics of useful financial information
- financial statements and the reporting entity
- the elements of financial statements
- recognition and derecognition
- measurement
- presentation and disclosure

The objective of financial reporting

Key Point

The objective of financial reporting is to provide information about the financial position, performance and changes in financial position of an entity that is useful to a wide range of users in making economic decisions.

In practice, this boils down to providing users with information about the entity's ability to generate cash.

Cash is not the same as profit. However, the statement of profit or loss provides an indication of the entity's ability to create wealth and, by implication, generate net cash from its operations so that it might pay dividends to its shareholders.

The statement of financial position contains a host of non-cash balances. However, the statement of financial position does give readers an indication of the capacity to generate cash by giving information about the resources available to the business and the manner in which they have been invested.

Qualitative characteristics of useful financial information

Key Point

Qualitative characteristics are the attributes that make the information provided in financial statements useful to users.

Fundamental characteristics:

- Relevance
- Faithful representation.

Enhancing characteristics:

- comparability
- verifiability
- timeliness
- understandability

Information can only be useful if it is material. Information is only material if its omission or misstatement could influence the decisions of users.

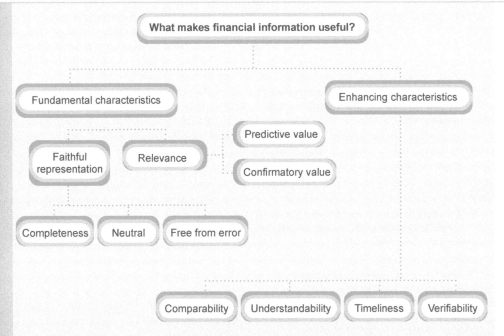

The elements of financial statements

Key Point

The definitions of the elements, particularly of assets and liabilities, are of fundamental importance. They determine the accounting treatment of a host of items in the financial statements.

Everything that is recognised in the financial statements can be classified in terms of one of the five elements as defined below.

Definition

'An asset is a present economic resource controlled by the entity as a result of past events' (Framework, para 4.3)

Note that ownership is not mentioned anywhere in the definition of assets. It is possible to obtain control without ever becoming the owner (e.g. through a lease agreement) and so some of an entity's assets could be owned by someone else.

Definition

'A liability is a present obligation of the entity to transfer an economic resource as a result of past events' (Framework, para 4.26).

Defining liabilities has been a major source of difficulty in the past. Companies have sought to identify ways of raising finance without having to recognise any liability in the statement of financial position ('off-balance sheet financing'). This definition could mean that a liability has to be recognised even though the entity does not 'owe' anything.

Key Point

All of the other definitions follow on from those for assets and liabilities.

Definition

'Equity is the residual interest in the assets of the entity after deducting all its liabilities' (Framework, para 4.63).

Assets = Equity + Liabilities
Equity = Assets – Liabilities

Definition

'Income is increases in assets or decreases in liabilities, that result in increases in equity, other than those relating to contributions from holders of equity claims' (Framework, para 4.68).

Definition

'Expenses are decreases in assets or increases in liabilities, that result in decreases in equity, other than those relating to distributions to holders of equity claims.' (Framework, para 4.69).

Recognition of the elements of financial statements

Elements are recognised if recognition provides users with useful financial information. In other words recognition must provide:

- relevant information

- a faithful representation of the asset or liability, and resulting income, expenses or equity movements.

Exam focus

Underpinning question practice

To practise the basics use the following test your understandings:

- Study Text Chapter 6
- Test your understanding 1
- Test your understanding 2
- Test your understanding 3
- Test your understanding 4
- Test your understanding 5

7

Conceptual framework – measurement

In this chapter

* Measurement in financial statements.

Measurement in financial statements

There are several bases for measuring the figures in financial statements. Some are in common use, while others are of a more theoretical nature.

Historical cost

Assets are valued in the statement of financial position at their initial cost.

Non-current assets are depreciated over time.

Fair value

The amount the item would realise in an orderly arm's length disposal.

Current cost

The cash that would be paid to replace the asset at current values, reflecting the asset's age and condition.

Value in use

The discounted value of future cash flows.

> **Key Point**
>
> In practice, financial statements are prepared using a combination of different measurement bases.
>
> In theory, it would be possible to develop a whole system of accounting that used one or other basis exclusively for all assets and liabilities.

Chapter 7

For example:

- inventory is valued at the lower of historical cost and net realisable value
- non-current assets are usually valued at either depreciated historical cost or their fair value
- impaired non-current assets are valued at either their value in use or their net realisable value.

Thus most assets are shown at their historical costs, but some are valued using an alternative basis.

In practice, financial statements will be deemed to have achieved these requirements if they:

- conform with accounting standards
- conform with the any relevant legal requirements
- have applied the qualitative characteristics from the Framework.

IAS 1 Presentation of Financial Statements requires that financial statements that have been prepared in accordance with IFRS Standards should disclose that fact.

Underpinning question practice

To practise the basics use the following test your understandings:

- Study Text Chapter 7
- Test your understanding 1

8

Other Standards

In this chapter

- IAS 8 Accounting polices, changes in accounting estimates and errors.
- IFRS 13 Fair value measurements.
- IAS 2 Inventory.
- IAS 41 Agriculture.

IAS 8 Accounting policies, changes in accounting estimates and errors

Exam focus

IAS 8 is an important standard because it clarifies the accounting treatment of a variety of accounting issues, including:

- selection of accounting policies
- changes in accounting policies
- changes in accounting estimates
- correction of prior period errors.

Accounting policies

Definition

Accounting policies are the principles, bases, conventions, rules and practices applied by an entity which specify how the effects of transactions and other events are reflected in the financial statements.

IAS 8 requires an enterprise to select and apply appropriate accounting policies complying with IFRS Standards and Interpretations to ensure that the financial statements provide information that is:

- relevant to the decision-making needs of users and
- represents faithfully the results and financial position of the entity.

```
                          ┌─────────────────┐
                          │      IAS 8      │
                          └─────────────────┘
```

Change in accounting policy	Change in accounting estimate	Errors
Retrospective treatment	Prospective treatment	Retrospective treatment
• New policy applied • Restate retained earnings • Disclose in SOCIE • Restate comparatives	• Change current and future periods • Disclose if change material	• Restate opening assets, liabilities and equity as if error never occurred • Adjust retained earnings • Disclose in SOCIE • Restate comparatives

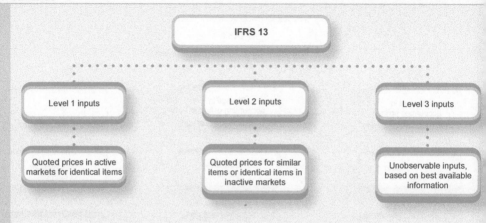

IAS 2 Inventory

> Inventory should be valued at the lower of

COST	NET REALISABLE VALUE (NRV)

Cost includes all costs incurred in bringing the inventory to its present location and condition

NRV = selling price less costs to sell/ complete

IAS 41 Agriculture

- Initially recognised at fair value less cost to sell.
- Revalue to fair value less costs to sell at year end.
- Take gain or loss to statement of profit or loss.

Exam focus

Exam standard questions on this area can be found in the exam kit as follows:

Objective case questions:

- Q286– 295

Underpinning question practice

- Study Text Chapter 8
- Test your understanding 1 – 3

9

Financial assets and financial liabilities

In this chapter

- Financial instruments.

Financial instruments

This has been a controversial area in practice. At one time there was a huge industry associated with the creation of complex financial instruments that had a distorting effect on the statements of financial position of the companies that used them.

Definition

A financial instrument is any contract that gives rise to a financial asset of one entity and a financial liability or equity instrument of another entity.

Financial liabilities

Key Point

The main problem has been that debt generally makes statements of financial position look weaker. In the past a great deal of ingenuity was put into the creation of financial statements that made debt less visible.

This improved gearing ratios, but in an artificial way because the company was liable for a higher debt than the statement of financial position acknowledged.

Key Point

At initial recognition a financial instrument should be measured at fair value. Thereafter all financial liabilities (other than liabilities held for trading and derivatives that are liabilities) should be measured at amortised cost using the effective interest rate method.

All financial liabilities within FR will be measured at amortised cost.

Liabilities that are issued at a discount or have issue costs associated with them are accounted for using amortised cost and the net cash will be recorded as the initial liability:

Nominal value of liability	X
Discount on issue	(X)
Issue costs	(X)
Initial liability	X

Amortised cost table:

Year	b/fwd	Finance cost (SPL) (effective interest rate)	Payment (nominal interest rate)	C/fwd (SFP)
1	X	X	(X)	X
2	X	X	(X)	X

Preference shares:

Irredeemable preference shares without mandatory dividend are treated as equity in the statement of financial position and any dividends paid are recorded as reductions in retained earnings and disclosed in the SOCIE.

Redeemable preference shares have characteristics of a liability and in substance are debt. These are therefore treated as financial liabilities in the statement of financial position and any dividends are recorded as finance costs. Use the amortised cost table to calculate the carrying amount for SFP and finance cost for SPL.

Compound instruments:

A compound instrument is one which has both a liability and an equity component and must be broken down between these components and shown separately in the statement of financial position.

The process to account for a convertible can be summarised as follows:

Step 1:	Value the debt at inception
	• this is done by finding the present value of the cash outflows (interest and capital repayment) using the market rate discount factor
Step 2:	Find the equity option
	• this is done by finding the residual amount between the cash received and the value of the liability at inception (from step 1). The equity option should be recorded in equity in the statement of financial position and disclosed in the SOCIE.
Step 3:	The debt element should now be accounted for at amortised cost as any other financial liability (use amortised cost table).

Financial assets

Key Point

Initial measurement of financial assets

All financial assets are to be measured initially at fair value.

Key Point

Subsequent measurement of financial assets

Subsequent measurement then depends upon whether the financial asset is an investment in a debt instrument or an equity instrument, as follows:

Debt instruments:

Debt instruments would normally be measured at fair value through profit or loss (FVPL), but could be measured at amortised cost if the entity chooses to do so, provided the following two tests are passed:

* business model test
* contractual cash flow characteristics test

Equity instruments:

Equity instruments are measured at:

* fair value through profit or loss (FVPL), or
* fair value through other comprehensive income (FVOCI) (if shares are not held for trading).

De-recognition issue 'Debt factoring'

Issue: Should this be treated as a separate sale of receivables or should it be treated as a loan secured on the receivables?

Exam standard questions on this area can be found in the exam kit as follows:

Objective case questions:

* Q301 – 325

Underpinning question practice

To practise the basics use the following test your understandings:

* Study Text – Chapter 9
* Test your understanding 1
  Test your understanding 2
  Test your understanding 3
  Test your understanding 4
  Test your understanding 5
  Test your understanding 6

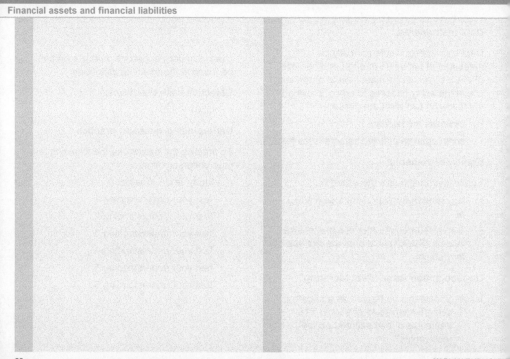

10

Foreign currency transactions

In this chapter

- Definitions.

Definitions

- Functional currency: **'The currency of the primary economic environment in which the entity operates'** (IAS 21, para 8).

- Presentation currency: **'The currency in which the financial statements are presented'** (IAS 21, para 8).

1. Initial treatment
   Translate using the historic rate prevailing at the transaction date

2. Settled Transaction
   If a transaction is settled during the accounting period

   - Translate at the date of payment using the historic rate prevailing at that date.

   - Any exchange gains or losses will be taken to the statement of profit or loss.

3. Unsettled transaction
   If transaction is unsettled at the reporting date, the treatment depends on whether the item is monetary or not.

   - If item is not a monetary item, leave at historic rate.

   - If item is monetary item, retranslate at closing rate.

   - Exchange differences will be posted to the statement of profit or loss.

Exam focus

Exam standard questions on this area can be found in the exam kit as follows:

Objective case questions:

Q326 – 328

Underpinning question practice:

- Study Text – Chapter 10
- Test your understanding 1 – 4

Revenue

In this chapter

- IFRS 15 Revenue from contracts with customers.
- Identifying performance obligations.

IFRS 15

Step 1 – Identify the contract

Step 2 – Identify the separate performance obligations within the contracts

Step 3 – Determine the transaction price

Step 4 – Allocate the transaction price to the performance obligations in the contract

Step 5 – Recognise revenue when (or as) a performance obligation is satisfied

Identifying performance obligations

If obligation settled at a point in time, recognise revenue at that point.

Specific Scenarios

1   Agency sales – Recognise commission only in revenue

2   Sale or return – If control over goods does not pass to the buyer, do not record any revenue

3   Sale and repurchase – If control over goods does not pass to the buyer, do not record any revenue. Treat 'proceeds' as loan and charge interest to date of repurchase.

If obligation settled over time, recognise over time:

- Record revenue and expenses based on progress
- For loss-making contracts, provide for full loss immediately
- If progress is unknown, recognise revenue to level of recoverable costs.

In statement of financial position:

- Record receivable if revenue exceeds amount received
- Record work-in-progress if cash spent exceeds cost of sales
- Record liability if cash received exceeds revenue
- Record provision if contract is loss making.

Exam kit:

Objective case questions:

- Q331 – 340

Underpinning question practice

- Study Text – Chapter 11

Test your understanding 1 – 11

12

Leases

In this chapter

- IFRS 16.

IFRS 16

If an entity has beneficial use of an asset under a leasing arrangement then both the asset and the liability must be recorded.

The only exceptions to this principle are leases of 12 months or less, or low-value assets.

Definitions

'A lease is a contract, or part of a contract, that conveys the rights to use an asset (the underlying asset) for a period of time in exchange for consideration' (IFRS 16, Appendix A).

A **lessor** is the entity that provides the right-of-use asset and, in exchange, receives consideration.

A **lessee** is the entity that obtains use of the right-of-use asset and, in exchange, transfers consideration.

A **right-of-use asset** represents the lessee's rights to use an underlying asset over the lease term.

Exam focus

Substance over form

The treatment required by IFRS 16 effectively accounts for the economic substance of leases rather than their legal form. The economic substance is that the lessee has the beneficial use of an asset and has an obligation to pay for that use. The fact that the lessee may never become the legal owner of the asset is irrelevant. We need to recognise both the asset and the liability.

Accounting for leases

Initial measurement

At the commencement of the lease, the lessee should recognise a lease liability and a right-of-use asset.

The lease liability is initially measured at the present value of the lease payments that have not yet been paid. The discount rate should be the rate implicit in the lease.

The right-of-use asset is initially recognised at cost, which comprises:

- The amount of the initial measurement of the lease liability
- Any lease payments made at or before the commencement date
- Any initial direct costs
- The estimated costs of removing or dismantling the underlying asset in accordance with the terms of the lease.

Subsequent measurement

Asset

The right-of-use asset is measured using the cost model (unless another measurement model is chosen). This means that it is measured at its initial cost less accumulated depreciation and impairment losses. The asset is depreciated over the shorter of the asset's useful life and the lease term, unless ownership of the asset transfers to the lessee at the end of the lease, in which case depreciation should be charged over the asset's useful life.

Liability

The liability is measured using amortised cost, which is the initial value plus any interest charged minus any payments made.

Within the FR exam you could be asked to calculate up to five figures for leased assets.

Statement of profit or loss

- Depreciation
- Finance cost

Statement of financial position

- Right-of-use asset
- Non-current lease liability
- Current lease liability

Read the details about the lease payments very carefully. In particular, make sure that you know whether the lease payments are in advance or in arrears. A lease liability table will help you calculate the finance cost and the split between current and non-current liability.

Rentals in advance

Year	Balance b/f	Rental paid	Net balance	Finance cost (SPL)	Balance c/f (SFP)
1	X	(X)	X	X	X
2	X	(X)	X*	X	X

Rentals in arrears

Year	Balance b/f	Finance cost (SPL)	Rental paid	Balance c/f (SFP)
1	X	X	(X)	X
2	X	X	(X)	X*

The lease liability at the end of Year 1 is split between non-current liability (NCL) and current liability (CL).

NCL is the balance remaining (*) immediately after Year 2's payment has been made. CL is the total Year 1 liability less NCL.

Sale and leaseback agreement

Is the transfer a sale under IFRS 15?

If not, continue to recognise the asset and treat the sale proceeds as a loan.

If the transfer is a sale, treat the asset as disposed and re-acquired as a new right-of-use asset. The gain to be recognised on disposal will be based on the proportion of asset rights transferred to the buyer.

Exam standard questions on this area can be found in the exam kit as follows:

Objective case questions:

*   Q296 – 305

Underpinning question practice

To practise the basics use the following test your understandings within Chapter 12 of the Study Text

*   Test your understanding 1

    Test your understanding 2

    Test your understanding 3

    Test your understanding 4

    Test your understanding 5

13

Taxation

In this chapter

- Income tax.
- Deferred tax.

Income tax

Standard income tax working:

Current year estimate	X
Under/over provision	X/(X)
Increase/decrease in deferred tax	X/(X)
Tax expense	$\overline{\underline{\text{X}}}$ →SPL

Deferred tax

Deferred tax arises because profits can be recognised for accounting purposes in one period and for tax in another.

> Definition

Deferred tax is the estimated future tax consequences of transactions and events recognised in the financial statements of the current and previous periods.

Deferred tax arises because of **temporary differences**.

The main cause of temporary differences in FR exam is:

Accelerated capital allowances mean that non-current assets are written off very quickly after purchase. That means that companies can claim a lot of tax relief when non-current assets are new, but relatively little when the assets are older.

In the short term more tax relief is claimed in the tax calculation than depreciation is charged in the statement of profit or loss. That difference is reversed in the longer term when depreciation catches up with the taxable capital allowances.

Accelerated capital allowances mean that tax on profit is delayed, so there is a **deferred tax liability**.

You may also see **deferred tax assets** arising as a result of temporary differences, where income or expenditure within the financial statements is recognised in a different year for taxation purposes.

Chapter 13

Deferred tax process:

Step 1: Calculate the temporary difference (or sometimes given)

It may be calculated as:

Carrying amount	X
Tax base	(X)
Temporary difference	X

Step 2: Apply the tax rate to the temporary difference to find the year end deferred tax liability (or is sometimes given). This liability is included in NCL in SFP.

Step 3: Account for the movement in deferred tax in tax expense (which is the difference between the opening DT liability (on trial balance) and closing DT liability (step 2)).

Exam standard questions on this area can be found in the exam kit within the published financial statements questions.

Objective case questions:

*   Q116 – 120
*   Q329 – 330

Constructed questions

Note that all CR questions covering financial statements preparation for single entities include taxation elements.

Underpinning question practice

To practise the basics use the following test your understandings:

*   Study Text – Chapter 13

    Test your understanding 1

    Test your understanding 2

    Test your understanding 3

    Test your understanding 4

14

Earnings per share

In this chapter

- Earnings per share.

Earnings per share (EPS)

Basic EPS calc:

$$\frac{\text{Earnings}}{\text{Shares}}$$

Exam focus

Basic EPS factors:

Full Market Issue – cash generated so weighted average table required.

Bonus Issue – no cash generated; weighted average table not required; assume takes place from day one.

Rights issue – combines characteristics of both a full market issue and a bonus issue – therefore a weighted average table required and the "free" shares following rights to be determined by:

- Calculating the ex-rights price (the share price after the rights issue)

- Then apply the rights issue bonus fraction to the shares in issue before the rights in the weighted average table.

$$\frac{\text{Actual cum rights price (given in Q)}}{\text{Theoretical ex rights price (calculated)}}$$

Key Point

Proforma weighted average table

Date	Actual number of shares	Fraction of year	Bonus fraction	Total
X	X	X	X	X

Diluted EPS

Diluted EPS calc:

$$\frac{\text{Earnings} + \text{Notional Extra Earnings}}{\text{Shares} + \text{Notional Extra shares}}$$

Chapter 14

Diluted EPS factors:

Convertibles – Calculated to show users of the accounts the potential impact upon conversion i.e. the interest payment would be saved (incurring extra tax) and the share capital would increase.

Options – Calculated to show users of the accounts the potential impact of the issue of future shares at a pre-determined price i.e. the difference between number of shares actually purchased and the amount that could be bought at fair value = "free" shares.

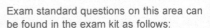

Exam standard questions on this area can be found in the exam kit as follows:

Objective case questions:

- Q341 – 345

Underpinning question practice

To practise the basics use the following test your understandings:

- Study Text – Chapter 14

  Test your understanding 1

  Test your understanding 2

  Test your understanding 3

  Test your understanding 4

  Test your understanding 5

  Test your understanding 6

  Test your understanding 7

15

Provisions, contingent liabilities and contingent assets

In this chapter

- Provisions.
- Contingent liabilities and contingent assets.
- Events after the reporting date.

Provisions

The accounting treatment of provisions is dealt with by IAS 37 Provisions, contingent liabilities and contingent assets.

Definition

'A provision is a liability of uncertain timing or amount' (IAS 37, para 10).

IAS 37 requires that a provision should be 'recognised when:

- an entity has a present obligation (legal or constructive) as a result of a past event
- it is probable that an outflow of resources embodying economic benefits will be required to settle the obligation, and
- a reliable estimate can be made of the amount of the obligation' (IAS 37, para 14).

Companies have, in the past, recognised provisions in order to smooth out reported earnings. Large provisions might be made in good years and then cancelled in bad years in order to create a steady trend in profits.

This is particularly true in the case of provisions for reorganisation. Before a provision can be made there has to be a detailed plan for the reorganisation and the company must have raised a valid expectation in those affected that it will take place (e.g. by issuing redundancy notices).

There is no formal definition of 'probable' but that is usually defined as "more likely than not", or even 50:50, in practice.

The amount recognised as a provision should be:

- a realistic estimate
- a prudent estimate of the expenditure needed to settle the obligation existing at the reporting date
- discounted back to net present value whenever the effect of this is material.

Contingent liabilities and contingent assets

IAS 37 also deals with this issue.

'A contingent liability is:

- a possible obligation that arises from past events and whose existence will be confirmed only by the occurrence or non-occurrence of one or more uncertain future events not wholly within the control of the entity, or
- a present obligation that arises from past events but is not recognised because:
  - it is not probable that an outflow of resources embodying economic benefits will be required to settle the obligation, or
  - the amount of the obligation cannot be measured with sufficient reliability' (IAS 37, para 10).

Contingent liabilities:

- should not be recognised in the statement of financial position itself
- should be disclosed in a note unless the possibility of a transfer of economic benefits is remote.

Definition

'A contingent asset is a possible asset that arises from past events and whose existence will be confirmed only by the occurrence or non-occurrence of one or more uncertain future events not wholly within the control of the enterprise' (IAS 37, para 10).

Contingent assets should not generally be recognised, but if the possibility of inflows of economic benefits is probable, they should be disclosed.

Events after the reporting date

IAS 10 *Events after the reporting date* distinguishes between adjusting and non-adjusting events.

Definition

Adjusting events are events after the reporting date which provide additional evidence of conditions existing at the reporting date.

Adjusting events require the adjustment of amounts recognised in the financial statements. For example, the discovery that a major trade receivable should be written off as a bad debt should be reflected in the relevant statement of profit or loss and statement of financial position figures.

Non-adjusting events are events after the reporting date which concern conditions that arose after the reporting date.

Non-adjusting events should be disclosed by note if they are of such importance that non-disclosure would affect the ability of the users of the financial statements to make proper evaluations and decisions. For example, an uninsured loss arising from a fire that occurred after the reporting date.

The note should disclose the nature of the event and an estimate of the financial effect, or a statement that such an estimate cannot be made.

Proposed dividends

Dividends proposed before but declared after the reporting date may not be included as liabilities at the reporting date.

The liability arises at the declaration date so they are non-adjusting events after the reporting date and must be disclosed by note as required by IAS 1.

Exam standard questions on this area can be found in the exam kit as follows:

Objective case questions:

• Q346 – 365

Underpinning question practice

To practise the basics use the following test your understandings:

• Study Text – Chapter 15
  Test your understanding 1
  Test your understanding 2
  Test your understanding 3
  Test your understanding 4
  Test your understanding 5

16

Statement of cash flows

In this chapter

- IAS 7 Statement of cash flows.
- Interpreting a statement of cash flows.

IAS 7 Statement of cash flows

Exam focus

Within FR students will not have to prepare a complete statement of cash flows, although extracts may be required as part of section C. Individual calculations may be required in sections A or B.

The statement of cash flows provides an important insight into the ways in which the entity has created and applied cash during the period. The fact that a business generated profit during a period means that it has created wealth, but wealth is not necessarily reflected by cash. The fact that a business is liquid according to the statement of financial position at the year end does not say a great deal about the cash movements that occurred during the year.

IAS 7 requires the provision of a cash flow statement that classifies cash flows into:

- operating activities
- investing activities
- financing activities.

The following pro-forma is useful for preparing a complete statement of cash flows:

Cash flows from operating activities

	$	$
Net profit before tax		X
Adjustments for:		
Interest expense (finance cost)	X	
Investment income	(X)	
Depreciation	X	
Profit on sale of non-current assets	(X)	
Increase in provisions	X	
Government grant amortisation	(X)	
Increase in accruals	X	
Increase in prepayments	(X)	
Increase in inventories	(X)	
Increase in trade receivables	(X)	
Increase in trade payables	X	
Cash generated from operations		X
Interest paid		(X)
Income taxes paid		(X)
Net cash from operating activities		X

Cash flows from investing activities:

	$	$
Purchases of property, plant and equipment	(X)	
Proceeds of sale of property, plant and equipment	X	
Interest received	X	
Government grants received	X	
Dividends received	X	
Net cash used in investing activities		(X)

Cash flows from financing activities:

Proceeds from issue of shares	X	
Proceeds from long-term borrowings	X	
Payment of lease liabilities	(X)	
Dividends paid	(X)	
Net cash used in financing activities		(X)
Net increase in cash and cash equivalents		X
Cash and cash equivalents at beginning of period		X
Cash and cash equivalents at end of period		X

This approach to calculating **cash generated from operations** is known as the "indirect method". It starts with profit before tax from the statement of profit or loss and:

- adjusts for interest and investment income to get back to profit from operations
- adjusts for non-cash items such as depreciation
- adjusts for increases and decreases in working capital.

The balancing figure approach is useful when balances are unknown in the question (such as tax paid, non-current asset purchases etc).

Proforma working example:

Tax payable

Balancing figure (β)= tax paid	X	B/f (SFP)	X
		Tax expense (SPL)	X
C/ f (SFP)	X		
	X		X

Or:

B/f tax payable (SFP)	X
Tax expense (SPL)	X
Tax paid (balancing figure (β))	(X)
C/f tax payable (SFP)	X

Approach to preparation of complete statement of cash flows

1. Read requirement, set up proforma answer and workings
2. Highlight notes and ref to FS's (look for easy cash balances that have already been given)
3. Cash and equivalent movement = easy mark
4. Go down proforma, starting with PBT
5. Tick each number as it is used

Interpreting a statement of cash flows

The statement of cash flows is a vital supplement to the other statements. Arguably, there is no point in a business existing if it cannot produce an adequate profit. However, cash can be more important in the short term because a business that runs short of cash could fail even if it has the capacity to generate profits and even return to a cash surplus in the longer term.

The statement of cash flows provides another dimension to the liquidity position shown in the statement of financial position.

Exam focus

You have to be careful not to make a hasty judgement about the net cash flow for the year.

It is not necessarily a good thing to generate a cash inflow or suffer a cash outflow. If a company is too liquid already then it would be better to invest in profit-making assets or to return the surplus funds to the shareholders as a dividend.

Similarly, raising cash is not an end in itself. It might be necessary to raise funds from borrowing, but the statement of cashflow should be read in conjunction with the statement of financial position to see what overall effect the changes during the year have had on the company's overall financial position.

You should also beware of short-term 'window-dressing' of the closing cash position. Delaying payments to suppliers and pressing customers for prompt payment can inflate cash balances (and improve some of the liquidity ratios) but the effects of this will disappear when the company returns to its normal practices after the reporting date.

Exam standard questions on this area can be found in the exam kit as follows:

Objective case questions:

- Q391 – 400

Underpinning question practice

To practise the basics use the following test your understandings:

- Study Text – Chapter 16

    Test your understanding 1

    Test your understanding 2

17

Principles of consolidated financial statements

In this chapter

- The concept of group accounts.
- Definition of a subsidiary.

The concept of group accounts

Group accounts could be examined as a 20 mark question in section C, either as a financial statements preparation or interpretation question.

A group comprises two or more companies that are controlled as a single economic entity.

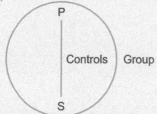

P & S are separate legal entities but in economic substance they are regarded as a single unit (a group).

Within the FR exam, a group may comprise a parent and up to two subsidiaries.

Group accounts combine the financial statements of the various group members and present the result as if the separate companies were a single economic entity.

This is logical because they are, by definition, all under the parent's control.

Applicable accounting standards

The following standards relate to the preparation of consolidated financial statements:

- IFRS 3 (Revised) Business combinations

- IFRS 10 Consolidated Financial Statements

- IAS 28 Investments in associates.

Chapter 17

Definition of a subsidiary

Subsidiary – 'an entity that is controlled by another entity' (IFRS 10, Appendix A).

Control – For examination purposes, control is usually established based on ownership of more than 50% of voting shares.

An investor controls an investee when:

- 'It has power over the investee
- It has exposure, or rights, to variable returns from its involvement with the investee
- It has the ability to use its power over the investee to affect the amount of the investor's returns' (IFRS 10, para 7).

Exemption from preparation of group financial statements

IFRS 10 Consolidated Financial Statements states that a parent need not present consolidated financial statements if and only if:

- the parent itself is a wholly owned subsidiary or a partially owned subsidiary
- the parent's debt or equity instruments are not traded in a public market
- the parent did not file its financial statements with a securities commission or other regulatory organisation
- the ultimate parent company produces consolidated financial statements that comply with IFRS Standards and are available for public use.

Excluded subsidiaries

It is generally not acceptable to exclude a subsidiary from the consolidated financial statements. The only exceptions are highly unlikely to occur in practice:

- on the basis of materiality
- the subsidiary might be held for resale.

Exam focus

You should understand the definition of a subsidiary in case the exam question asks you to justify the decision to include or exclude a particular company from the group accounts.

Consolidated statement of financial position

In this chapter

- The basic principle.
- Basic workings.
- Intra-group trading adjustments.
- Fair values.
- Mid-year acquisitions.

The basic principle

Key Point

The basic principle running through the whole topic of consolidation is:

- cancel all balances that exist between group members and
- combine the remaining figures so that
- the resulting totals show the assets and liabilities controlled by the group.

Exam focus

A good technique is to create a pro-forma, inserting the 'easy' numbers, then complete the workings to calculate the additional numbers required.

Basic workings

There are 5 standard workings for CSFP.

Regardless of the difficulty of the question, having a process to work through will help you tackle a group accounting question.

Where there is more than one subsidiary, separate workings 2, 3 and 4 will be required for each subsidiary.

Set out your workings as follows:

W1 Group structure

```
                        P
Date of acquisition     |    >50%
                        S
```

(W2) Net assets of S

	At acquisition	At reporting date	Post acquisition
Share capital	X	X	
Share premium	X	X	
Retained earnings	X	X	X
FV adjustment	X	X	
FV depreciation		(X)	(X)
PUP (sub = seller)		(X)	(X)
Uniform accounting policy adjustment	X	X	
	___	___	___
	X	X	X

(W3) Goodwill

Parent holding (investment) at fair value	X
NCI value at acquisition (*)	X
	X
Less	
Fair value of net assets at acquisition (W2)	(X)
Goodwill to date on acquisition	X
Impairment	(X)
Carrying amount of goodwill	X ⟶ CSFP

(*) If fair value method adopted, NCI value = fair value of NCI's holding at acquisition (number of shares NCI own × subsidiary share price).

(*) If proportion of net assets method adopted, NCI value = NCI % × fair value of net assets at acquisition (from W2).

(W4) Non-controlling interest

NCI value at acquisition (as in W3)	X
NCI share of post-acquisition reserves (W2)	X
NCI share of impairment (fair value method only)	(X)
	X $\longrightarrow$ CSFP

(W5) Group retained earnings

100% P's retained earnings	X
P's % impairment of goodwill	(X)
PUP (P= seller)	(X)
Unwinding of the discount	(X)
Acquisition costs	(X)
P's % of S post-acq profit	X
P's % of A post-acq profit	X
Impairment of associate	(X)
PUP (P or A = seller)	(X)
	X $\longrightarrow$ CSFP

Intra-group trading adjustments

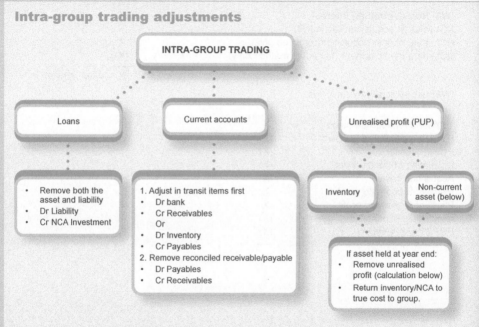

INTRA-GROUP TRADING

Loans

Current accounts

Unrealised profit (PUP)

- Remove both the asset and liability
- Dr Liability
- Cr NCA Investment

1. Adjust in transit items first
   - Dr bank
   - Cr Receivables
   Or
   - Dr Inventory
   - Cr Payables
2. Remove reconciled receivable/payable
   - Dr Payables
   - Cr Receivables

Inventory

Non-current asset (below)

If asset held at year end:
- Remove unrealised profit (calculation below)
- Return inventory/NCA to true cost to group.

Calculation of unrealised profit

- Inventory – use cost structures (mark-up or margin)
- Non-current asset transfers:

Assume that the asset had never been transferred i.e. put the asset back to the group value and remove the unrealised profit element split between original profit, adjusted in the seller (debit), and excess depreciation, adjusted in the buyer (credit).

Carrying amount with transfer	X
Carrying amount without transfer	X
Diff = unrealised profit	X

Accounting for PUP

- If parent = seller
  Dr Group retained earnings (W5)   X
  Cr Inventory/NCA in CSFP   X
  Cr Net assets (W2) at reporting
  date (for NCA)   X

- If subsidiary = seller
  Dr Net assets (W2) at reporting date   X
  Cr Inventory/NCA in CSFP   X
  Cr Group retained earnings (W5)
  (for NCA)   X

Pay particular attention to the wording of the question when calculating the unrealised profit. Small changes to the wording can affect the way in which this profit is calculated.

Fair values

To ensure that an accurate figure is calculated for goodwill and that group assets/ liabilities are correctly calculated and valued in the consolidated financial statements, fair values must be used.

Cost of investment

The consideration paid for a subsidiary must be accounted for at fair value.

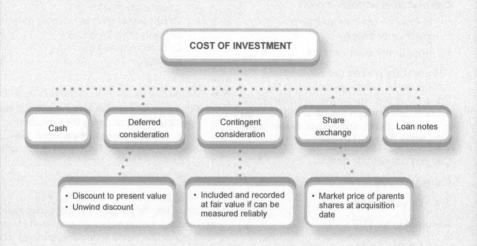

Often in the exam, the parent company has only recorded the cash consideration. If prompted, ensure you record the shares/ liabilities as these represent valuable marks.

Subsidiary's net assets

The subsidiary's identifiable assets and liabilities acquired must be accounted for at their fair values:

- Update W2 net assets
- Update assets/liabilities in consolidated statement of financial position.

Also remember to update for any extra FV depreciation since acquisition.

Mid-year acquisitions

If an acquisition takes place during the year then the net assets as at the date of acquisition must be estimated.

This might involve assuming that the profit or loss of the subsidiary accrued evenly throughout the year so as to determine retained earnings at acquisition to be used in W2.

IFRS 3 Business Combinations

Goodwill treatment

- Positive
  - Capitalise
  - Annual impairment tests
- Negative
  - Check calculations
  - Never capitalised
  - Credit to the statement of profit or loss

- Acquisition costs
  - Expense immediately (deduct in W5)

Question approach

- Read requirement, set up pro-forma answer
- Add line by line down the SFP's – every number goes somewhere!
- Complete workings
  1. Group structure
  2. S's NAs
  3. Goodwill
  4. NCI
  5. Group RE
  6. Investment in A (chapter 20)

Proforma CSFP

Assets

NCA

PPE (P + S + FV adj – FV dep adj)	X
Goodwill (W3)	X
Investment in associate (W6)	X
	X

CA

Inventories (P + S – PUP + inventory in transit)	X
Receivables (P + S – intra-group receivable)	X
Cash (P + S + cash in transit)	X
Total Assets	X

Equity and liabilities

Share capital (P only) (P + unrecorded share exchange)	X
Share premium (P only) (P + unrecorded share exchange)	X
Group retained earnings (W5)	X
NCI (W4)	X

NCL

Borrowings (P + S + unrecorded deferred consideration + unwinding of discount)   X

CL

Payables (P + S – intra-group payable) $\underline{X}$

Total equity & liabilities $\underline{\underline{X}}$

Exam focus

Exam standard questions on this area can be found in the exam kit as follows:

Objective case questions:

- Q366 – 380

Constructed response questions:

- December 2014 – Plastik
- December 2011 – Paladin
- September/December 2015 – Palistar

Underpinning question practice

- To practise the basics use the following test your understandings:
- Study Text
- Chapter 18
- Test your understanding 4
- Test your understanding 5
- Test your understanding 6
- Test your understanding 7
- Test your understanding 8

19

Consolidated statement of profit or loss

In this chapter

- The basic principles.
- Basic workings for a consolidated statement of profit or loss.
- Mid-year acquisitions.

The basic principles

There are three basic principles:

- Adjust for any intra-group items such as sales or dividends.
- From revenue to profit for the year include all of P's income and expenses plus all of S's income and expenses and if any other comprehensive income add all of P's other income to all of S's other income (to reflect control of S).
- After total comprehensive income firstly show split of profit between amounts attributable to the parent's shareholders and the non-controlling interest and then show split of total comprehensive income between amounts attributable to the parent's shareholders and non-controlling interest (to show ownership).

The important thing is to read the question very carefully in order to decide which adjustments affect the balance brought forward on the retained earnings as opposed to those that affect the profit for the year.

Basic workings for a consolidated statement of profit or loss

There are 2 basic workings for CSPL

W1 Group structure

W2 Non-controlling interest

This is calculated by:	
Subsidiary's profit for year	X
less:	
Fair value depreciation	(X)
PUP (sub = seller only)	(X)
Impairment	
(fair value method only)	(X)
	X
x NCI% =	X

The 5 standard working approach (seen in chapter 18) is not required for the consolidated statement of profit or loss itself. However, often exam questions where the primary content is a consolidated statement of profit or loss will require a calculation of goodwill or non-controlling interest at the reporting date – therefore your standard CSFP workings may still be needed.

Adjustments

Just like the consolidated statement of financial position there are often intra-group items to be adjusted for:

```
                        INTRA GROUP ITEMS
```

Sales and purchases	Interest (on intra-group loans)	Dividends	PUP
Remove transfer price from both revenue and cost of sales	Remove interest received and paid from finance costs and investment income	Remove dividends received by parent from subsidiary (from investment income)	Once calculated add onto cost of sales
			if sub = seller also update NCI working (W2)

Mid-year acquisitions

- Pro-rate S's results on a line by line basis
- Pro-rate share of profit in NCI working (W2)

Additional group expenditure

- Impairment
  - Add to expenses
  - Update NCI working (if fair value method used)
- Fair value depreciation
  - Add extra depreciation to cost of sales
  - Update NCI working
- Unwinding discounts
  - Add to finance costs

Be wary in the exam of additional group expenditure and follow examiner specific instructions e.g. if the examiner states fair value depreciation should be included in cost of sales ensure it is added there.

Question approach:

- Read requirement, set up answer and workings
- Line by line (P + S) – every number goes somewhere!
- Adjustments
- Complete workings
  - NCI
  - Share of A's profits (chapter 20)

Proforma consolidated statement of profit or loss and other comprehensive income

Revenue (P + S – intra-group sales)	X
COS (P + S – intra group purchases + PUP + FV depn)	(X)
Gross profit	X
Operating costs (P + S + goodwill impairment)	(X)
Profit from operations	X
Finance costs (P + S + unwinding – intra-group interest charge)	(X)
Investment income (P + S – intra-group interest income – div from S)	X
Profit from associate (W3)	X
Profit before tax	X
Tax (P + S)	(X)
Profit for the year	X
Other comprehensive income	
Revaluation gain (P + S)	X
Total comprehensive income	X

Profit attributable to:	
P's shareholders (β)	X
NCI (W2)	X
	X
Total comprehensive income attributable to:	X
P's shareholders (β)	X
NCI ((W2) + % S's comprehensive income)	X
	X

Exam standard questions on this area can be found in the revision kit as follows:

Objective case questions:

- Q371 – 375

Constructed response questions:

- December 2013 – Polestar
- June 2014 – Penketh
- December 2016 – Laurel

Underpinning question practice

To practise the basics use the following test your understandings:

- Study Text
- Chapter 19
- Test your understanding 1
- Test your understanding 2
- Test your understanding 3
- Test your understanding 4
- Test your understanding 5

Associates

In this chapter

- IAS 28 Investments in associates.
- Equity accounting.
- Equity accounting: further aspects.

IAS 28 Investments in associates

Definition

'**An associate is an entity over which the investor has significant influence**' (IAS 28, para 3).

'**Significant influence is the power to participate in the financial and operating policy decisions of the investee but is not control or joint control over those policies**' (IAS 28, para 3).

Exam focus

The definition of significant influence is very broad. You might have to read the question very carefully in order to decide whether an investment creates an associate.

It is normally assumed that significant influence exists if the holding company has a shareholding of 20% to 50%. That does not, however, guarantee that the holding company has any real influence. For example, a 40% shareholding might actually offer very little real influence if the remaining 60% is in the hands of another individual shareholder.

Equity accounting

Key Point

The holding company is not required to produce consolidated statements unless it has at least one subsidiary. Associates are accounted for using equity accounting within the consolidated financial statements, but the existence of an associate does not, in itself, require the preparation of group accounts.

Equity accounting in the consolidated statement of financial position

- Remove the non-current asset investment in parent's books relating to the associate.
- Do NOT consolidate line-by-line.
- Calculate the 'Investment in associate' to be included in the group financial statements using a new working:

W6 Investment in associate

Cost of investment	X
P's % of associate post-acq profit	X
P's Impairment	(X)
P's % of PUP	(X)
	X → CSFP

- Bring P's % of associate's post-acquisition profits into consolidated statement of financial position via W5.

Equity accounting in the consolidated statement of profit or loss

- Remove any dividends received by the parent from the associate.
- Do NOT consolidate line-by-line.
- Bring in parent's 'share of associate' for the year using a new working:

W3 P's % of A's profits

P's % of associate profit for the year (Time apportion if mid-year acquisition in period)	X
Impairment	(X)
P's % of PUP	(X)
	X → CSPL

Associates are not members of the group in the same way that subsidiaries are.

Always remember that subsidiaries are **controlled** by the holding company, whereas associates are subject to no more than **significant influence**.

Equity accounting: further aspects

Fair values

If the fair value of the associate's net assets at acquisition are materially different from their book value the net assets should be adjusted in the same way as for a subsidiary.

Balances with the associate

Generally the associate is considered to be outside the group. Therefore balances between group companies and the associate will remain in the consolidated statement of financial position.

If a group company trades with the associate, the resulting payables and receivables will remain in the consolidated statement of financial position.

Sales to and from associates

Sales between group members and associates are left in the consolidated statement of profit or loss. The only adjustments are in respect of any closing inventory that remains from such transactions.

Unrealised profit in inventory

Unrealised profit in closing inventory arising from sales between group members and associates should still be eliminated, but only adjust for P's % of PUP.

Where parent sells to associate

In CSFP
Dr Group retained earnings (W5)
Cr Investment in associate (W6)

In CSPL
Add to cost of sales

Where associate sells to parent

In CSFP
Dr Group retained earnings (W5)
Cr Inventory (on face of CSFP)

In CSPL
Deduct from share of associate profit

Ensure you only remove the associates % of PUP, e.g. 30%.

Exam standard questions on this area can be found in the exam kit as follows:

Constructed response questions:

- December 2016 – Laurel
- June 2012 – Pyramid

Consolidated statement of profit or loss

- December 2009 – Pandar
- December 2012 – Viagem

Underpinning question practice

To practise the basics use the following test your understandings:

- Study Text Chapter 20
- Test your understanding 1
- Test your understanding 2
- Test your understanding 3
- Test your understanding 4
- Test your understanding 5

chapter

21

Disposals

In this chapter

- Parent company financial statements.
- Consolidated financial statements.

Parent company financial statements

In parent company financial statements:

Proceeds	X
Carrying amount of investment	(X)
Gain/loss on disposal	X/(X)

The investment may be held at cost or at fair value in the parent's financial statements, depending on its classification as an equity investment.

Consolidated financial statements

In consolidated financial statements:

Sale proceeds		X
Net assets at date of disposal	X	
Net goodwill at date of disposal	X	
NCI at date of disposal	(X)	
		(X)
Gain/loss on disposal		X

Goodwill at disposal date can be calculated using the standard goodwill working used in the preparation of a consolidated statement of financial position.

In calculating net assets at disposal date, profits may need to be pro-rated to find retained earnings at date of disposal.

Non-controlling interest at date of disposal can be valued using fair value method or proportion of net assets method.

Chapter 21

Other considerations

The results of the subsidiary must be consolidated up to the date of disposal in the statement of profit or loss. This can be consolidated line by line or shown separately as a discontinued operation.

Exam focus

The FR exam may contain a subsidiary disposal as part of a consolidated statement of profit or loss question, in which case it should be treated as a discontinued operation.

See the Exam Kit question Zeffer for practice in this area.

22

Interpretation of financial statements

In this chapter

- Analysing financial statements.

Analysing financial statements

Exam focus

A 20 mark question could potentially deal with the appraisal of performance.

Exam focus

There are probably more marks available for interpreting ratios in the exam than for their calculation.

Perspective

There is always a reason for interpreting accounting information. The purpose of the analysis will determine its focus and the depth. A bank manager thinking of extending a short-term overdraft facility might be interested in liquidity whereas a shareholder might be more interested in profitability.

Exam focus

Always read the question carefully and ensure that any position or perspective is taken into account in choosing and discussing ratios.

Sounding professional

The following hints and tips are based on many years of examining and marking for professional bodies.

- Know what each ratio means. If, for example, you know what the gross profit percentage is then you will not really need to memorise the formula. You will also find it easier to comment sensibly on the results.

- Look at the numbers before you calculate any ratios. If one company's revenue is three times the other's then it might have advantages in terms of economies of scale that could affect your analysis.

- Organise the ratios into groups and deal with them in a logical sequence. Profitability is usually more important than liquidity or gearing, so start with that. The return on capital employed is by far the most important profitability ratio. Good answers usually start with return on capital employed, then the secondary profitability ratios, then move on to liquidity and gearing.

- Round sensibly. Percentages should be rounded off to whole numbers, as should days in the working capital ratios. The liquidity ratios can go to one decimal place.

- Don't exaggerate minor differences. If two companies have ratios that differ by a single percentage point then it is probably better to describe them as "similar" rather than building a case that one is better.

- If the numbers don't make sense then your calculations might be wrong.

Remember that the accounts are meant to present a realistic case. If receivables are settling their balances within three days then you might have miscalculated the ratio.

- Justify your assertions. Don't say 'this company's ratio is higher and that makes it better'. Explain why the higher ratio is beneficial.

- Look for relationships between ratios. Try to demonstrate some commercial awareness. If, for example, a company has a healthy gross profit percentage and also spends a large proportion of its revenue on selling and distribution then it might be worth suggesting that the success in sales is partly due to investing in advertising.

Ratio calculations

Profitability	Liquidity	Gearing	Investor
• ROCE	• Current ratio	• Gearing	• EPS
• Gross profit	• Quick ratio	• Interest cover	• Dividend yield
• Operating profit	• Inventories days		• Dividend cover
• Asset turnover	• Receivables days		• P/E ratio
	• Payables days		

Profitability

$$\text{ROCE} = \frac{\text{PBIT}}{\text{Capital Employed (Equity + Debt)}} \times 100\%$$

$$\text{Gross profit margin} = \frac{\text{Gross profit}}{\text{Revenue}} \times 100\%$$

$$\text{Operating profit margin} = \frac{\text{PBIT}}{\text{Revenue}} \times 100\%$$

$$\text{Asset turnover} = \frac{\text{Revenue}}{\text{Capital Employed}}$$

Short-term liquidity

Current ratio = $\dfrac{\text{Current Assets}}{\text{Current liabilities}}$:1

Quick ratio = $\dfrac{\text{Current Assets} - \text{Inventory}}{\text{Current liabilities}}$:1

Efficiency ratios (working capital)

Inventory days = $\dfrac{\text{Inventories}}{\text{COS}} \times 365$ days

Trade receivables collection period = $\dfrac{\text{Trade receivables}}{\text{Revenue}} \times 365$ days

Trade payables collection period = $\dfrac{\text{Trade payables}}{\text{Purchases (or COS)}} \times 365$ days

Long-term solvency

Gearing = $\dfrac{\text{Debt}}{\text{Equity}} \times 100\%$ or $\dfrac{\text{Debt}}{\text{Debt} + \text{Equity}} \times 100\%$

Interest cover = $\dfrac{\text{Profit before interest and tax}}{\text{Interest}}$ = times p.a.

Investor ratios

EPS = $\dfrac{\text{Earnings}}{\text{Shares}}$

Dividend yield = $\dfrac{\text{Dividend per share}}{\text{MV per share}} \times 100\%$

Dividend cover = $\dfrac{\text{PAT}}{\text{Dividend}}$

P/E ratio = $\dfrac{\text{Price per share}}{\text{Earnings per share}}$

Question approach:

1. Read requirement, look for headings for answer

2. Skim Q, look for absolute movements, get big picture and key info

3. Calculate ratios

4. Comment on ratios, use clues from Q, use headings and short paragraphs

 Exam focus

Exam standard questions on this area can be found in the exam kit as follows:

Objective case questions:

* Q381 – 390

Constructed response questions:

* June 2014 – Woodbank
* June 2015 – Yogi
* Non-exam – Flash Co
* September/December 2021 Pinardi Co

Underpinning question practice

To practise the basics use the following test your understandings:

* Study Text – Chapter 22

  Test your understanding 1

  Test your understanding 2

  Test your understanding 3

References

The Board (2022) *The Conceptual Framework* London: IFRS Foundation

The Board (2022) *IAS 2 Inventories* London: IFRS Foundation

The Board (2022) *IAS 7 Statement of Cash Flows* London: IFRS Foundation

The Board (2022) *IAS 8 Accounting Policies, Change in Accounting Estimates and Errors* London: IFRS Foundation

The Board (2022) *IAS 10 Events after the Reporting Period* London: IFRS Foundation

The Board (2022) *IAS 12 Income Taxes* London: IFRS Foundation

The Board (2022) *IAS 16 Property, Plant and Equipment* London: IFRS Foundation

The Board (2022) *IAS 20 Accounting for Government Grants and Disclosure of Government Assistance* London: IFRS Foundation

The Board (2022) *IAS 21 The Effects of Changes in Foreign Exchange Rates* London: IFRS Foundation

The Board (2022) *IAS 23 Borrowing Costs* London: IFRS Foundation

The Board (2022) *IAS 28 Investments in Associates and Joint Ventures* London: IFRS Foundation

The Board (2022) *IAS 33 Earnings per Share* London: IFRS Foundation

The Board (2022) *IAS 37 Provisions, Contingent Liabilities and Contingent Assets* London: IFRS Foundation

The Board (2022) *IAS 40 Investment property* London: IFRS Foundation

The Board (2022) *IAS 41 Agriculture* London: IFRS Foundation

The Board (2022) *IFRS 3 Business Combinations* London: IFRS Foundation

The Board (2022) *IFRS 5 Non-current Assets Held for Sale and Discontinued Operations* London: IFRS Foundation

The Board (2022) *IFRS 9 Financial Instruments* London: IFRS Foundation

The Board (2022) *IFRS 10 Consolidated Financial Statements* London: IFRS Foundation

The Board (2022) *IFRS 13 Fair Value Measurement* London: IFRS Foundation

The Board (2022) *IFRS 15 Revenue from Contracts with Customers* London: IFRS Foundation

The Board (2022) *IFRS 16 Leases* London: IFRS Foundation

Index

A

Accounting policies 50
Adjusting events 86
Amortise 21
Analysing financial statements 132
Asset 42

B

Basic EPS 80
Bonus Issue 80

C

Cash generating units 27
Changes in accounting estimates 50
Changes in accounting policies 50
Conceptual framework 38
Contingent asset 86
Contingent liabilities and contingent assets 85
Contingent liability 85
Control 99

D

Deferred tax 76
Depreciation 11
Diluted EPS 80
Discontinued operations 31

E

Earnings per share 80
Economic value 46
Elements 42
Elements of financial statements 42
Equity 43
Equity accounting 122
Events after the reporting period 86
Expenses 43

F

Fair value 46
Full Market Issue 80
Functional currency 62

G

Gain on revaluation 13

H

Held for sale 30
Historical cost 46

I

IAS 1 Presentation of financial statements 2, 47
IAS 2 Inventory 53
IAS 7 Statement of cash flows 90
IAS 8 accounting policies, changes in accounting estimates and errors 50
IAS 10 Events after the reporting date 86
IAS 16 Property, plant and equipment 10
IAS 20 Accounting for government grants and disclosure of government assistance 14
IAS 23 Borrowing costs 14
IAS 28 Investments in associates 98
IAS 33 Earnings per share 79
IAS 36 Impairment of assets. 25

IAS 37 Provisions, contingent liabilities and contingent assets 84
IAS 38 Intangible assets 20
IAS 40 Investment properties 15
IAS 41 Agriculture 53
IASB 35
IFRS 3 (Revised) Business combinations 98
IFRS 5 Non-current assets held for sale and discontinued operations 30
IFRS 13 Fair Value Measurement 52
IFRS 15 Revenue from contracts with customers 66
IFRS 16 Leases 70
Impairment 26
Income 43
Income tax 76
International Accounting Standards Board 34
Intra-group Trading 106
Investment property 15

L

Leases 70
Liability 42
Loss on revaluation 13

N

Net realisable value 46
Non-adjusting events 87
Not-for-profit and public sector entities 37

O

Objective of financial statements 39

P

Presentational currency 62
Principles-based v rules-based accounting 36
Provisions 83
PUP 107

Q

Qualitative characteristics 40

R

Ratio calculations 134
Recognition 43
Recoverable amount 26
Regulatory framework 36
Replacement cost 46
Research and development 21
Right-of-use asset 70
Rights issue 80
Rules v principles 36

S

Sale and repurchase 66
Significant influence 122
Statement of changes in equity 4, 5
Statement of financial position 3
Subsidiary 99